AGES *of* MAN

Sir John Gielgud's

AGES *of* MAN

SELECTIONS FROM
SHAKESPEARE

with

Commentary by
SIR JOHN GIELGUD

Introduction by
THOMAS LASK

CAEDMON
NEW YORK

H

Photograph of Sir John Gielgud © Bern Schwartz

Biography of William Shakespeare by G.B. Harrison from
The Penguin Shakespeare series, used with the kind permission of
Penguin Books Ltd., Middlesex, England

LC #: 78-741962
ISBN: 0-89845-009-8

All the world's a stage ...

—*As You Like It*

SIR JOHN GIELGUD (he was knighted in 1953) has been
acclaimed for more than four decades as one of the
foremost Shakespearean actors on the English-speaking
stage. And at least one of his roles, that of Hamlet, has
been compared with the historic performances of the
past. The noted director Tyrone Guthrie said of it: "It
was the most musical and the most royal. He was the
most satisfying embodiment of the part." Although the
characters Gielgud has played have ranged from
Benedick in "Much Ado About Nothing" to Prospero in
"The Tempest," he will surely be best remembered for
the darker and more somber roles: Macbeth, Lear,
Richard II, Angelo in "Measure for Measure" and of
course Hamlet, a part he has played more than 500
times.

Sir John would not on the face of it appear to be the
ideal Elizabethan performer. He is not of imposing
physical presence and by and large does not try to
overpower or storm his way through a role. He learned
his limitations early. When he was at school at the Royal
Academy of Dramatic Art—he reported later—"I
strained every fiber in my efforts to appear violent or
emotional, and only succeeded in forcing my voice and
striking strange attitudes with my body."

Nor is his voice of exceptional quality. It is musical
rather than resonant, lyrical and supple rather than
robust, though in the theater it has surprising carrying
power. But he has compensated for these seeming

shortcomings by an absolute mastery over the
Shakespeare line, by an ability to extract every bit of its
music and to render the speeches with utmost
intelligence. Critics have praised the "intellectual
lucidity" and "the extraordinary grace and winged
intelligence" of his playing. And he has been praised too
for the quick spontaneity of his readings, almost, it was
suggested, as if he were inventing the lines the poet had
given him to speak.

His clarity and simplicity were not achieved without
effort: "When I was young," he remarked once, "I
thought it was important to achieve effect rather than
truth. Today, the moment I feel I've got a performance,
I immediately start to take things away from it. I try to
use less voice, less gesture, less physical effort. I try to
make it more and more relaxed. I try to see each word I
speak in the air."

It must not be assumed that because his name is
most closely linked with Shakespeare he has completely
avoided the contemporary theater. In his early twenties,
under the guidance of the noted director and scenic
designer Theodore Komisarjevsky, Sir John got to know
the works of Chekhov when the Russian playwright
was not as popular as he is today. Over the years he has
appeared in "The Seagull," "The Cherry Orchard,"
"Three Sisters" and "Ivanov." He has also played other
Elizabethans besides Shakespeare as well as Congreve,
Ibsen, Sheridan. His version of Oscar Wilde's "The
Importance of Being Earnest," which he directed and in
which he played John Worthing, was the highlight of

the 1947 New York season. One reviewer thought
that it *was* the New York season.

And although it is easy to overlook, he has also
done a number of new plays. They have ranged from
Noel Coward's "The Vortex" in the 1920's to Harold
Pinter's "No Man's Land" in the 1970's, an arc that
almost encompasses the history of the theater in those
decades. In between there have been appearances in
O'Neill's "The Great God Brown," Edward Albee's
"Tiny Alice," "Home" by David Storey, and most
recently as Shakespeare himself in Edward Bond's bitter
drama about the poet's last years, "Bingo."

Gielgud's involvement in the theater has been
complete: he has been a producer and director as well as
a player. It has also been lifelong. He had the sense, as
has been remarked, to be born into a theatrical family.
His grandmother was Kate Terry, herself a well-known
Shakespearian actress before her early retirement. His
great aunt was Ellen Terry, his cousin the innovative and
influential scene designer Gordon Craig. Sir John was
born in 1904 into a comfortable family. His father,
Frank,was a stockbroker, but an amateur pianist of some
ability with a great interest in the theater. The boy had
already been to the theater by the time he was seven.
His initial interest, however, was not in acting but in
stage design. He recalled, "I developed a passion for
painting backcloths and designs in pastels for my toy
theater, and I felt sure I was destined to be a stage
designer." His father pointed out that to be a stage
designer, one would have to study architecture and that

in turn demanded a certain proficiency in math—a proficiency John never attained. Instead, after finishing at Winchester, the young man waived going to the university and enrolled in Lady Benson's School where he remained for three years. (He always retained, though, a very keen interest in scene design and its effects, as his writings show, and he remains a Sunday painter of watercolors. This interest extends as well to costumes, not only their cut, color and style, but also their psychological effect. He once wrote that it was "more important for costume to make the actor feel the part than look the part.") Two years at the Royal Academy of Dramatic Art followed during which he came under the tutelage of Claude Rains. In that time he got walk-ons and small roles. He was a spear holder in "Henry V" and an orderly in John Drinkwater's "Robert E. Lee." Then at age 19 and at the Old Vic he played Romeo to Gwen Flancon-Dacies's Juliet, his first major role. A year later he understudied and replaced Noel Coward in the latter's play "The Vortex," a considerable achievement for a young man. In the next decade he played with the Old Vic (Antony, Hotspur, Prospero) and in a number of classical and new plays elsewhere, including one season in which he alternated with Laurence Olivier as Romeo and Mercutio. Finally in 1934 he electrified theatergoers on both continents with his Hamlet, first on London's West End and two years later on Broadway, in Guthrie McClintic's production with Lillian Gish as Ophelia and Judith Anderson as the Queen.

It was this Hamlet that remains vivid in the minds of those who saw it. "Such a voice, such diction, and such a gift of maintaining the melody of Shakespeare's verse even while keeping it edged from speech to speech with dramatic significance, is a new experience," wrote the critic John Mason Brown. It was a Hamlet who was vulnerable, hurt, anguished. This theatergoer remembers the wistfulness in the voice that masked the pain within. And he recalls too the heartbreak of the parting from his mother at the end of the closet scene. And yet it was also a Hamlet that revealed different sides of the character: the sardonic, mocking, furious sides. "It was so vivid and alive that the play might have been written yesterday," was one final judgment.

A host of other memorable roles followed in due course after Hamlet: an especially beautiful Richard II, an icy Angelo in "Measure for Measure," a witty and rather sophisticated Benedick, and the great tragic roles of Macbeth and Lear.

In 1956 the British Arts Council asked Sir John to do an evening of poetry. He proposed instead an evening of Shakespeare and when the Council agreed, called George Rylands, who had directed him in productions of "Hamlet" and "The Duchess of Malfi," to work out the text. Rylands suggested that he use selections from Rylands's newly compiled anthology which in outline resembled what Gielgud was looking for. At first he appeared with a lutenist, a combination that did not seem to sit well with his hearers. Eventually he dropped the musician and changed the selections until they were closer to what he originally had had in mind.

"I felt here was an opportunity to show myself to
the present generation in parts in which I had been a
success, things I'd played and loved when I was young.
And then I added some of the sonnets and poems to
give the whole thing a leavening."

He played it all over Europe and Great Britain as
"The Ages of Man" with great success. In America,
where he brought it in 1958, it won special praise. On
opening night the actor received such an ovation as to
bring tears to his eyes. "A masterpiece," Brooks
Atkinson, the drama critic of The New York Times, called
it. It was a remarkable feat to sustain an evening in the
theater purely on the strength of the lines without props,
except for a lectern and a book which was almost never
consulted, and with no elaborate lighting. There were
no costumes, no scenery and the actor himself wore a
dinner jacket. Yet it was an evening of hypnotic power.

In a way it is easy to see why. For in "The Ages of
Man," Shakespeare and Gielgud's special gifts were
joined in perfect harmony. For him the lines had always
been foremost: the rhythm, the sound, the imagery, the
shadings they were capable of. The strengths of his
performances had always been anchored in the words.
He conveyed not only their meanings but those con-
notative qualities, those overtones that enhance our
pleasure in Shakespeare. Hear for example what he does
with "eternal" in the line "But thy eternal summer shall
not fade" in Sonnet 18, and how he handles the diph-
thongs and open vowels in Lorenzo's speech from "The

Merchant of Venice." Consider too the virtuosity with which he manages the pauses, caesuras and run-ons in the long Queen Mab speech from "Romeo and Juliet."

"There is no life except in the play," he once remarked. The statement is an index to his style. There is no before or after. He never asks how many children Lady Macbeth had nor does he try for deeper psychological probing than Shakespeare provided. Even when he is stripped of virtually all the trappings of the theater, Sir John is still in his element. Sense and sound become one and the listener feels that there is no barrier between him and the poet. It is hard to believe that the art of communication can go any further.

THOMAS LASK

CONTENTS

Manhood

WAR   CIVIL STRIFE   KINGSHIP
GOVERNMENT AND SOCIETY   PASSION AND CHARACTER

Age

DEATH   SICKNESS   MAN AGAINST HIMSELF
OLD AGE   TIME

Youth

CHILDHOOD   MAGIC *and* FAERY

NATURE   LOVE

JEALOUSY

LUST

FOR HIS ANTHOLOGY of selections from Shakespeare, Sir
John Gielgud has divided his gathering into three parts:
"Youth," "Manhood" and "Age." The selections are not
in a narrow sense descriptions of these periods. They
are rather expressions of the feelings, the passions, the
problems of the spirit that characterize these times:
youth with its passionate and lyrical attitude to love and
life; manhood with its jockeying for power; age with its
concern with death and the unchangeable past.
Compare, for example, the glow, the warmth and the
ardor of Lorenzo's speech, "How sweet the moonlight
sleeps upon this bank" in the opening section with the
autumnal, resigned and melancholy strain of the song
from "Cymbeline," "Fear no more the heat o' th' Sun,"
in the last section. A whole lifetime can be squeezed
between these sets of verses.

The very first speech, the famous lines of Jaques
from "As You Like It," serves as an epigraph to the
entire book, making physical growth and decline the
metaphorical equivalent of the waxing and waning of
the mind. But with the selection from "A Midsummer
Night's Dream" we are free of age altogether and are in
the natural world. The passage that begins "I know a
bank where the wild thyme blows" is the voice of the
poet who knew the countryside and loved it. The scene
may be fairyland, but the brooks and flowers are
English.

The madcap fancy and fooling of the "Queen Mab" speech from "Romeo and Juliet" is not only an exercise in the fantastic, but the expression of the high spirits of a young man intoxicated with his own wit. It is almost as if Mercutio, having latched on to an idea, would not let it go until he had extracted every bit of fun from it.

"Romeo and Juliet" is the quintessential romantic play and Sir John's choice of lines conveys the self-centered passion of the young lover, who in an environment hostile enough to lead to his death, thinks only of the young girl he has just met at the Capulet ball. The words he speaks are magical in the way they reflect the extravagance of the boy's own feelings:

> It seems she hangs upon the cheek of night,
> Like a rich jewel in an Ethiop's ear:
> Beauty too rich for use, for earth too dear:

But we know that love takes other forms: lust, jealousy and a kind of mocking indifference to the loved one that hides the truer feelings of the heart. Leontes's "Too hot, too hot:" shows a man caught in a web of his own making. The lines have a staccato beat; and the repeated rhetorical questions only increase his jealous misery. Leontes is as impermeable to calm reflection in his way as Romeo is to his.

On the other hand, the addition of reason, that ability to step outside oneself for an objective look, is what makes Angelo's speech from "Measure for Measure" so absorbing. He can feel his almost unnatural desire, but he is curious as to its nature and its course. "Is

this her fault, or mine?" he asks himself. And goes on:
"Most dangerous/Is that temptation, that doth goad us
on/To sin, in loving virtue." The tone is contemplative,
almost as if it were all happening to someone else. The
last lines are Angelo's rueful acknowledgment: "Ever till
now/When men were fond, I smil'd, and wonder'd
how."

Benedick, in his speech from "Much Ado," thinks he
is being reasonable when he is only being gulled. He
believes himself the master of his feelings and the
situation. But behind the bravado we sense a young
man waiting to be taken. His show of independence is
as hollow as a reed. It's a funny passage, doubly so to
those who know the outcome of the play.

Throughout the anthology Sir John scattered a
number of sonnets to lighten and leaven the text, as he
put it. They do more, however. For one, they are
beautiful in themselves, full of uncounted felicities, the
154 sonnets Shakespeare wrote making up very likely
the most sustained and accomplished sequence in that
form. The form attracted him as it has poets from its
introduction into England in the 16th century to World
War I when its popularity declined. The Elizabethans
loved it and poured out sonnets by the score. Petrarch,
who made the short lyric form popular, used an eight-
line opening that set forth the situation in the poem and
a six-line conclusion that resolved it. Shakespeare
adopted an alternate form, introduced by Wyatt and
Surrey, consisting of three quatrains and a rhymed
couplet at the end to drive the point home.

Taken all in all, Shakespeare in his sonnets shows himself to be an impatient craftsman. A number of the sonnets start strongly and finish lamely. But when he was young he liked the sonnet form well enough to work it into his plays. "Love's Labor's Lost" has seven, and there are two in "Romeo and Juliet." At their best, which is often enough, his sonnets rank among the finest of their kind.

Sir John has used the sonnets here to point up the text, sometimes to comment on it. The first two sonnets urge a young man to marry and have children, for he will age like all mankind—a notion to which youth gives only a quick and passing thought. The sonnet "My mistress' eyes are nothing like the sun" is an echo of the pretended indifference of Benedick's speech. Sonnet 129, "The expense of spirit in a waste of shame," is one of the most powerful in English. Standing as it does between Leontes's speech of jealous passion and Angelo's of icy lust, it makes an ironic commentary on both. For the sonnet argues that the pleasure they strain for is an illusion, "Before, a joy propos'd; behind, a dream." The very pursuit is "perjur'd, murd'rous, bloody, full of blame," and the poem nails the point home with as harsh a judgment as was ever made against man's animal spirit:

> *All this the world well knows; yet none knows well*
> *To shun the heaven that leads men to this hell.*

AS YOU LIKE IT   Act II, Scene 7

JAQUES:

All the world's a stage,
And all the men and women, merely Players;
They have their exits and their entrances,
And one man in his time plays many parts,
His Acts being seven ages. At first the infant,
Mewling, and puking in the nurse's arms:
And then the whining school-boy with his satchel
And shining morning face, creeping like snail
Unwillingly to school. And then a lover,
Sighing like furnace, with a woeful ballad
Made to his mistress' eyebrow. Then, a soldier,
Full of strange oaths, and bearded like the pard,
Jealous in honour, sudden, and quick in quarrel,
Seeking the bubble reputation
Even in the cannon's mouth: and then, the justice,
In fair round belly, with good capon lin'd,
With eyes severe, and beard of formal cut,
Full of wise saws, and modern instances,
And so he plays his part. The sixth age shifts
Into the lean and slipper'd pantaloon,
With specacles on nose, and pouch on side,
His youthful hose well sav'd, a world too wide
For his shrunk shank, and his big manly voice,
Turning again toward childish treble, pipes
And whistles in his sound. Last scene of all,
That ends this strange eventful history,
Is second childishness, and mere oblivion,
Sans teeth, sans eyes, sans taste, sans everything.

Shakespeare's sonnets are written some to a man, his friend and patron, and others to a dark lady. Here he writes to the man imploring him to marry and beget children.   J. G.

SONNET 2

When forty winters shall besiege thy brow
And dig deep trenches in thy beauty's field,
Thy youth's proud livery, so gaz'd on now,
Will be a tatter'd weed of small worth held:
Then being ask'd where all thy beauty lies,
Where all the treasure of thy lusty days,
To say within thine own deep-sunken eyes
Were an all-eating shame and thriftless praise.
How much more praise deserv'd thy beauty's use,
If thou couldst answer, "This fair child of mine
Shall sum my count and make my old excuse,"
Proving his beauty by succession thine.
　　This were to be new made when thou art old,
　　And see thy blood warm when thou feel'st it cold.

SONNET 12

When I do count the clock that tells the time,
And see the brave day sunk in hideous night;
When I behold the violet past prime,
And sable curls all silver'd o'er with white;
When lofty trees I see barren of leaves,
Which erst from heat did canopy the herd,

And summer's green all girded up in sheaves
Borne on the bier with white and bristly beard,
Then of thy beauty do I question make,
That thou among the wastes of time must go,
Since sweets and beauties do themselves forsake
And die as fast as they see others grow;
    And nothing 'gainst Time's scythe can make defence
    Save breed, to brave him when he takes thee hence.

A MIDSUMMER NIGHT'S DREAM   Act II, Scene 1

Oberon, King of the Faeries in A MIDSUMMER NIGHT'S
DREAM...   J.G.

OBERON:
  My gentle Puck come hither; thou rememb'rest
  Since once I sat upon a promontory,
  And heard a mermaid on a dolphin's back,
  Uttering such dulcet and harmonious breath,
  That the rude sea grew civil at her song,
  And certain stars shot madly from their spheres,
  To hear the sea-maid's music. ....

  That very time I saw (but thou couldst not)
  Flying between the cold Moon and the Earth,
  Cupid all arm'd; a certain aim he took
  At a fair Vestal, throned by the west,
  And loos'd his love-shaft smartly from his bow,
  As it should pierce a hundred thousand hearts:

But I might see young Cupid's fiery shaft
Quench'd in the chaste beams of the watery Moon;
And the imperial Votaress passed on,
In maiden meditation, fancy-free.
Yet mark'd I where the bolt of Cupid fell:
It fell upon a little western flower;
Before, milk-white; now purple with love's wound,
And maidens call it, love-in-idleness.
Fetch me that flower; the herb I shew'd thee once,
The juice of it, on sleeping eye-lids laid,
Will make or man or woman madly dote
Upon the next live creature that it sees.
Fetch me this herb, and be thou here again,
Ere the leviathan can swim a league. ....

Having once this juice,
I'll watch Titania, when she is asleep,
And drop the liquor of it in her eyes:
The next thing that she waking looks upon,
She shall pursue it, with the soul of love. ....

I know a bank where the wild thyme blows,
Where oxlips and the nodding violet grows,
Quite over-canopied with luscious woodbine,
With sweet musk-roses, and with eglantine;
There sleeps Titania, sometime of the night,
Lull'd in these flowers, with dances and delight:
And there the snake throws her enamell'd skin,
Weed wide enough to wrap a fairy in.
And with the juice of this I'll streak her eyes,
And make her full of hateful fantasies.

THE TEMPEST   Act III, Scene 2

In THE TEMPEST, *his last play, he surprises us with an equally magical speech, this time from the mouth of Caliban, the most debased and earthbound character in the play.*   J. G.

CALIBAN:

Be not afeard, the Isle is full of noises,
Sounds, and sweet airs, that give delight and hurt not:
Sometimes a thousand twangling instruments
Will hum about mine ears; and sometimes voices,
That if I then had wak'd after long sleep,
Will make me sleep again, and then in dreaming,
The clouds methought would open, and show riches
Ready to drop upon me, that when I wak'd
I cried to dream again.

ROMEO AND JULIET   Act I, Scene 4

Mercutio, the swaggering daredevil friend, chaffs the lovesick Romeo on their way to the Capulets' ball.   J. G.

MERCUTIO:

O then I see Queen Mab hath been with you:
She is the Fairies' midwife, and she comes
In shape no bigger than an agate-stone,
On the forefinger of an alderman,
Drawn with a team of little atomies,
Athwart men's noses as they lie asleep:
Her waggon-spokes made of long spinners' legs:

The cover, of the wings of grasshoppers,
The traces of the smallest spiders web,
The collars of the moonshine's watery beams,
Her whip of cricket's bone, the lash of film,
Her waggoner, a small grey-coated gnat,
Not half so big as a round little worm,
Prick'd from the lazy finger of a maid.
Her chariot is an empty hazel-nut,
Made by the joiner squirrel or old grub,
Time out o' mind, the Fairies' coachmakers:
And in this state she gallops night by night,
Through lovers' brains, and then they dream of love,
O'er courtiers' knees, that dream on court'sies straight,
O'er lawyers' fingers who straight dream on fees,
O'er ladies' lips who straight on kisses dream,
Which oft the angry Mab with blisters plagues,
Because their breaths with sweetmeats tainted are.
Sometime she gallops o'er a courtier's nose,
And then dreams he of smelling out a suit:
And sometime comes she with a tithe-pig's tail,
Tickling a parson's nose as a' lies asleep,
Then dreams he of another benefice.
Sometime she driveth o'er a soldier's neck,
And then dreams he of cutting foreign throats,
Of breaches, ambuscadoes, Spanish blades:
Of healths five fathoms deep, and then anon
Drums in his ear, at which he starts and wakes,
And being thus frighted, swears a prayer or two
And sleeps again: this is that very Mab
That plats the manes of horses in the night:

And bakes the elf-locks in foul sluttish hairs,
Which once untangled, much misfortune bodes.
This is the hag, when maids lie on their backs,
That presses them and learns them first to bear,
Making them women of good carriage:

THE MERCHANT OF VENICE   Act V, Scene 1

Lorenzo in THE MERCHANT OF VENICE, *who has eloped with Jessica, Shylock's daughter, walks with her by moonlight in the garden of Belmont.*   J.G.

LORENZO:
How sweet the moonlight sleeps upon this bank,
Here will we sit, and let the sounds of music
Creep in our ears; soft stillness, and the night
Become the touches of sweet harmony:
Sit Jessica, look how the floor of heaven
Is thick inlaid with patens of bright gold,
There's not the smallest orb which thou behold'st
But in his motion like an angel sings,
Still quiring to the young-eyed cherubins;
Such harmony is in immortal souls,
But whilst this muddy vesture of decay
Doth grossly close it in, we cannot hear it: ...

The man that hath no music in himself,
Nor is not moved with concord of sweet sounds,
Is fit for treasons, stratagems, and spoils,

The motions of his spirit are dull as night,
And his affections dark as Erebus,
Let no such man be trusted: mark the music.

MUCH ADO ABOUT NOTHING   Act II, Scene 3

But in a very different mood, Benedick, the woman-hater in MUCH
ADO ABOUT NOTHING, *muses on the sudden passion of his young
friend Claudio, who appears to have fallen violently in love.*   J.G.

BENEDICK:

I do much wonder, that one man seeing how much
another man is a fool, when he dedicates his
behaviours to love, will after he hath laugh'd at such
shallow follies in others, become the argument of his
own scorn, by falling in love, and such a man is
Claudio. I have known when there was no music for
him but the drum and the fife, and now he had rather
hear the tabor and the pipe: I have known when he
would have walk'd ten mile a-foot, to see a good
armour, and now will he lie ten nights awake carving
the fashion of a new doublet: he was wont to speak
plain, and to the purpose (like an honest man and a
soldier), but now is he turn'd orthograper, his words
are a very fantastical banquet, just so many strange
dishes: may I be so converted and see with these
eyes? I cannot tell, I think not: I will not be sworn but
love may transform me into an oyster, but I'll take

my oath on it, till he have made an oyster of me, he
shall never make me such a fool: one woman is fair,
yet I am well, another is wise, yet I am well: another
virtuous, yet I am well: but till all graces be in one
woman, one woman shall not come in my grace: rich
she shall be that's certain, wise, or I'll none, virtuous,
or I'll never cheapen her: fair, or I'll never look on
her, or come not near me, noble, or not I for an angel,
of good discourse, an excellent musician, and her hair
shall be of what colour it please God.

Two sonnets: one to love, and one to married love.   J. G.

SONNET 18

Shall I compare thee to a summer's day?
Thou art more lovely and more temperate:
Rough winds do shake the darling buds of May,
And summer's lease hath all too short a date:
Sometime too hot the eye of heaven shines,
And often is his gold complexion dimm'd;
And every fair from fair sometimes declines,
By chance, or nature's changing course, untrimm'd;
But thy eternal summer shall not fade
Nor lose possession of that fair thou ow'st,
Nor shall Death brag thou wand'rest in his shade
When in eternal lines to time thou grow'st:
   So long as men can breathe or eyes can see,
   So long lives this, and this gives life to thee.

SONNET 116

Let me not to the marriage of true minds
Admit impediments. Love is not love
Which alters when it alteration finds,
Or bends with the remover to remove:
O no! it is an ever-fixed mark,
That looks on tempests and is never shaken;
It is the star to every wandering bark,
Whose worth's unknown, although his height be
   taken.
Love's not Time's fool, though rosy lips and cheeks
Within his bending sickle's compass come;
Love alters not with his brief hours and weeks,
But bears it out even to the edge of doom:
   If this be error and upon me proved,
   I never writ, nor no man ever loved.

*But Shakespeare could sometimes be quite cynical, even on this
important subject.*   J. G.

SONNET 130

My mistress' eyes are nothing like the sun;
Coral is far more red than her lips' red;
If snow be white, why then her breasts are dun;
If hairs be wires, black wires grow on her head:
I have seen roses damask'd red and white,

But no such roses see I in her cheeks;
And in some perfumes is there more delight
Than in the breath that from my mistress reeks:
I love to hear her speak, yet well I know
That music hath a far more pleasing sound:
I grant I never saw a goddess go,
My mistress, when she walks, treads on the ground.
    And yet, by heaven, I think my love as rare
    As any she belied with false compare.

ROMEO AND JULIET

*Romeo sees Juliet at the Capulets' ball, falls in love with her and stands
beneath her balcony.*   J.G.

Act I, Scene 5

ROMEO:

What Lady's that which doth enrich the hand of
yonder knight? ...

O she doth teach the torches to burn bright:
It seems she hangs upon the cheek of night,
Like a rich jewel in an Ethiop's ear:
Beauty too rich for use, for earth too dear:
So shows a snowy dove trooping with crows,
As yonder Lady o'er her fellows shows.
The measure done, I'll watch her place of stand,
And touching hers, make blessed my rude hand.
Did my heart love till now, forswear it sight,
For I ne'er saw true beauty till tonight.

Act II, Scene 1

   Can I go forward when my heart is here,
   Turn back dull earth and find thy centre out.

Act II, Scene 2

   But soft, what light through yonder window breaks?
   It is the East, and Juliet is the Sun.
   Arise fair Sun and kill the envious Moon,
   Who is already sick and pale with grief,
   That thou her maid art far more fair than she:
   Be not her maid since she is envious,
   Her vestal livery is but sick and green,
   And none but fools do wear it, cast it off:
   It is my Lady, O it is my love,
   O that she knew she were,
   She speaks, yet she says nothing, what of that?
   Her eye discourses, I will answer it:
   I am too bold, 'tis not to me she speaks:
   Two of the fairest stars in all the heaven,
   Having some business, do intreat her eyes,
   To twinkle in their spheres till they return.
   What if her eyes were there, they in her head,
   The brightness of her cheek would shame those
     stars,
   As daylight doth a lamp, her eye in heaven
   Would through the airy region stream so bright,
   That birds would sing, and think it were not might:
   See how she leans her cheek upon her hand.
   O that I were a glove upon that hand,
   That I might touch that cheek. ....

She speaks.
Oh speak again bright Angel, for thou art
As glorious to this night being o'er my head,
As is a winged messenger from heaven
Unto the white-upturned wondering eyes,
Of mortals that fall back to gaze on him,
As he bestrides the lazy puffing clouds,
And sails upon the bosom of the air.

THE WINTER'S TALE   Act I, Scene 2

King Leontes of Sicilia, in THE WINTER'S TALE, *is obsessed by the conviction that his friend, Prolixenes, is the lover of his wife, Queen Hermione.*   J.G.

LEONTES:

Too hot, too hot:
To mingle friendship far, is mingling bloods.
I have *tremor cordis* on me: my heart dances,
But not for joy; not joy. This entertainment
May a free face put on: derive a liberty
From heartiness, from bounty, fertile bosom,
And well become the agent: 't may; I grant:
But to be paddling palms, and pinching fingers,
As now that are, and making practis'd smiles
As in a looking-glass; and then to sigh, as 'twere
The mort o' th' deer; oh, that is entertainment
My bosom likes not, nor my brows. ....

Is whispering nothing?
Is leaning cheek to cheek? is meeting noses?
Kissing with inside lip? stopping the career
Of laughter, with a sigh? (a note infallible
Of breaking honesty) horsing foot on foot?
Skulking in corners? wishing clocks more swift?
Hours, minutes? noon, midnight? and all eyes
Blind with the pin and web, but theirs; theirs only,
That would unseen be wicked? Is this nothing?
Why then the World, and all that's in 't, is nothing,
The covering sky is nothing, Bohemia nothing,
My wife is nothing, nor nothing have these
  nothings,
If this be nothing.

SONNET 129

Th' expense of spirit in a waste of shame
Is lust in action; and till action, lust
Is perjur'd, murd'rous, bloody, full of blame,
Savage, extreme, rude, cruel, not to trust;
Enjoy'd no sooner, but despised straight;
Past reason hunted; and no sooner had,
Past reason hated as a swallow'd bait
On purpose laid to make the taker mad:
Mad in pursuit, and in possession so;
Had, having, and in quest to have, extreme;
A bliss in proof, and prov'd, a very woe;
Before, a joy propos'd; behind, a dream.

All this the world well knows; yet none knows
 well
To shun the heaven that leads men to this hell.

MEASURE FOR MEASURE   Act II, Scene 2

Angelo, the prim, self-righteous deputy in MEASURE FOR
MEASURE, *as Isabella the novice begs him for her brother's life,
suddenly begins to realize that he himself is guilty of the very vice he
most condemns.*   J. G.

ANGELO:

　What's this? what's this? is this her fault, or mine?
　The tempter, or the tempted, who sins most? ha?
　Not she: nor doth she tempt: but it is I,
　That, lying by the violet in the sun,
　Do as the carrion does, not as the flower,
　Corrupt with virtuous season: Can it be,
　That modesty may more betray our sense
　Than woman's lightness? having waste ground
　 enough,
　Shall we desire to raze the Sanctuary
　And pitch our evils there? oh fie, fie, fie:
　What dost thou? or what art thou Angelo?
　Dost thou desire her foully, for those things
　That make her good? oh, let her brother live:
　Thieves for their robbery have authority,
　When Judges steal themselves: what, do I love her,
　That I desire to hear her speak again?
　And feast upon her eyes? what is't I dream of?

O cunning enemy, that to catch a Saint,
With Saints dost bait thy hook: most dangerous
Is that temptation, that doth goad us on
To sin, in loving virtue; never could the strumpet
With all her double vigour, art, and nature
Once stir my temper; but this virtuous maid
Subdues me quite: Ever till now
When men were fond, I smil'd, and wonder'd how.

Manhood

WAR   CIVIL STRIFE

KINGSHIP

GOVERNMENT *and* SOCIETY

PASSION *and* CHARACTER

MANHOOD BRINGS us to the heart of political power: how
men attain it, how they retain it, and what kind of men
they are. In the plays such matters turn on kingship, on
those who hold the crown and on those who wish to
wrest it from them. What emerges are not tracts of
political science, but superb portraits of human beings
often caught up in events larger than themselves, who
are unable to measure up to what is demanded of them,
and those who bend destiny to their own purposes. The
way for all of them in the chronicle plays and the
tragedies is never smooth: "Uneasy lies the head, that
wears a crown." But whether they are saints or villains
or mere mortals like us, Shakespeare, with a kind of
Jovian understanding, draws them all as human beings.

Hotspur, whose magnificent and revealing speech is
the second item in this section, was after all a rebel. He
was threatening the rule of Henry IV and his action
carried with it all the promises of civil strife. The
Elizabethans, with the memory of the war between the
houses of Lancaster and York still fresh in their minds,
would not have taken a rosy view of a rebel in the
making. And from what we can gather from
Shakespeare's attitude to mobs and crowds, he probably
did not approve either. And yet when he came to write
about Hotspur, how forthright and winning he made
him. As the words pour out of Hotspur in his desire to

reply to the king's charge of disobedience, he stands
revealed as a gallant, open, uncalculating soldier,
especially so in contrast to the careful Prince Hal, who
never quite forgets the gap between himself and his
low-born companions. Hotspur's speech could not be
more vivid in summoning up the scene on the
battlefield, his own weariness, the arrival of the
perfumed, fastidious fop who would have taken to arms
were it not for the guns involved. To read this
marvelous speech aright requires both clarity and speed,
almost as if it were one seamless ribbon of sound. Sir
John's handling of the lines is masterly.

In the fourth selection we are in the middle of a
scene in which the man who has just been challenged
by Hotspur is in the process of deposing his own
monarch. The focus is on the king, the weak, posturing
Richard II, as much interested in the histrionics of his
position as in the loss of power. Richard starts off
defiantly enough. There is a divinity that hedges a king,
he argues; he is the annointed of the Lord and so on.
But as he is compelled to give up the throne, he relishes
more and more the opportunities for dramatic display,
asking Henry to hold the other side of the crown, and
for a glass to behold his own piteous image. The entire
passage from the outrage at the beginning to the tearful
self-pity at the end is like a novella, dominated by one
character.

The remaining passages in "Manhood" are variations
on the above theme. The speech of Henry VI, which in
its repetitions and slow rhythm gives the passage a slow,

pastoral air, offers us a picture of a man who has the crown and does not want it. In the mouths of some other monarchs, Henry's lines would sound hypocritical. In the mouth of this weak though saintly king, they express true yearning.

Cassius, as we can tell from his speech, is the very antithesis of the powerless Henry. For he is the true conspirator: jealous, ambitious, one who measures himself against his adversary and does not find himself wanting. More, he is quite willing to hazard his future by his actions. Yet the whole speech in which he tries to convince Brutus that Caesar is as mortal and as vulnerable as they are is ironic. Because it is Brutus who undermines the conspiracy by his lack of firmness. He yields when he should be ruthless. It might be said that Cassius's speech is almost too successful.

The selection is a good example of what Shakespeare can do with a narrative passage. The lines have a propulsive force; there are few end-stopped lines. The language is plain, unadorned and fluid. Monosyllables abound. In one four-line stretch there are only two words of more than one syllable. Everything conspires to hasten the verse along and to give a breathless urgency to the events in the speech and to Cassius's own telling of these events.

Hamlet's soliloquy, "Oh what a rogue and peasant slave am I," is cast in personal terms. He upbraids himself for delinquent behavior. Yet that speech too is about power and the obligations of power even though these obligations have been thrust on him. Hamlet's self-flagellation, no matter how poetically expressed, cannot hide his delinquency. And though he is light-years away from Hotspur—who would not have hesitated a second in dispatching Claudius—both are goaded by the same spur: the sense that their honor has been violated and they must set it right.

                                                                                    T. L.

46 St.

SIR
JOHN
GIELGUD
"AGES OF MAN"

Measure For Measure: *What's this? what's this? is this her fault, or mine?*
The tempter, or the tempted, who sins most? ha?

Much Ado About Nothing: *...I will not be sworn but love may transform me into an oyster...*

Hamlet: *To be, or not to be, that is the question...*

The Tempest:...*we are such stuff*
As dreams are made on; and
our little life
Is rounded with a sleep.

King Lear: *Howl, howl, howl, howl: O you men of stone...*

Julius Caesar: *Cowards die many times before their deaths, The valiant never taste of death but once...*

HENRY THE FIFTH   Prologue

PROLOGUE:

O for a Muse of Fire, that would ascend
The brightest Heaven of invention:
A Kingdom for a stage, Princes to act,
And Monarchs to behold the swelling scene.
Then should the warlike Harry, like himself,
Assume the port of Mars, and at his heels
(Leash'd in, like hounds) should Famine, Sword,
  and Fire
Crouch for employment. But pardon, gentles all,
The flat unraised spirits, that have dar'd,
On this unworthy scaffold, to bring forth
So great an object. Can this cock-pit hold
The vasty fields of France? Or may we cram
Within this wooden O the very casques
That did affright the air at Agincourt?
O pardon: since a crooked figure may
Attest in little place a million,
And let us, ciphers to this great accompt,
On your imaginary forces work.
Suppose within the girdle of these walls
Is now confin'd two mighty Monarchies,
Whose high, upreared, and abutting fronts,
The perilous narrow Ocean parts asunder.
Piece out our imperfections with your thoughts:
Into a thousand parts divide one man,
And make imaginary puissance.
Think when we talk of horses, that you see them,
Printing their proud hoofs i' th' receiving earth:

For 'tis your thoughts that now must deck our
   Kings,
Carry them here and there: jumping o'er times;
Turning th' accomplishment of many years
Into an hour-glass: for the which supply,
Admit me Chorus to this History;
Who prologue-like, your humble patience pray,
Gently to hear, kindly to judge our play.

HENRY THE FOURTH (PART I)   Act I, Scene 3

In HENRY THE FOURTH (PART I), *young Harry Percy, known as
Hotspur, defends himself against a charge of insubordination at the
Battle of Holmedon.*   J. G.

HOTSPUR:
  My liege, I did deny no prisoners,
  But I remember when the fight was done,
  When I was dry with rage, and extreme toil,
  Breathless and faint, leaning upon my sword,
  Came there a certain Lord, neat and trimly dress'd,
  Fresh as a bridegroom, and his chin new reap'd,
  Show'd like a stubble-land at harvest home,
  He was perfumed like a milliner,
  And 'twixt his finger and his thumb he held
  A pouncet box, which ever and anon
  He gave his nose, and took 't away again,
  Who therewith angry, when it next came there

Took it in snuff, and still he smil'd and talk'd:
And as the soldiers bore dead bodies by,
He call'd them untaught knaves, unmannerly,
To bring a slovenly unhandsome corse
Betwixt the wind and his nobility:
With many holy-day and lady terms
He questioned me, amongst the rest demanded
My prisoners in your Majesty's behalf.
I then, all smarting with my wounds being cold,
To be so pester'd with a popinjay,
Out of my grief and my impatience
Answer'd neglectingly, I know not what
He should, or he should not, for he made me mad
To see him shine so brisk, and smell so sweet,
And talk so like a waiting gentlewoman,
Of guns, and drums, and wounds, God save the
  mark:
And telling me the sovereignest thing on earth
Was parmaceti, for an inward bruise,
And that it was great pity, so it was,
This villainous saltpetre, should be digg'd
Out of the bowels of the harmless earth,
Which many a good tall fellow had destroyed
So cowardly, and but for these vile guns
He would himself have been a soldier.
This bald unjointed chat of his (my Lord)
I answered indirectly (as I said)
And I beseech you, let not his report
Come current for an accusation
Betwixt my love and your high majesty.

HENRY THE SIXTH (PART 3)   Act II, Scene 5

But if Shakespeare loves his braggarts and warriors, how tenderly he deals with his weaker heroes. King Henry the Sixth laments the responsibilities of kingship and longs for the imagined joys of a pastoral life.   J.G.

HENRY:

Oh God! methinks it were a happy life,
To be no better than a homely swain,
To sit upon a hill, as I do now,
To carve out dials quaintly, point by point,
Thereby to see the minutes how they run:
How many makes the hour full complete,
How many hours brings about the day,
How many days will finish up the year,
How many years, a mortal man may live.
When this is known, then to divide the times:
So many hours, must I tend my flock;
So many hours, must I take my rest:
So many hours, must I contemplate:
So many hours, must I sport myself:
So many days, my ewes have been with young:
So many weeks, ere the poor fools will ean:
So many months, ere I shall shear the fleece:
So minutes, hours, days, months, and years,
Pass'd over to the end they were created,
Would bring white hairs, unto a quiet grave.
Ah! what a life were this? How sweet? how lovely?
Give not the hawthorn bush a sweeter shade
To shepherds looking on their silly sheep,
Than doth a rich embroider'd canopy

To Kings, that fear their Subjects' treachery?
Oh yes, it doth; a thousand-fold it doth.
And to conclude, the shepherd's homely curds,
His cold thin drink out of his leather bottle,
His wonted sleep, under a fresh tree's shade,
All which secure, and sweetly he enjoys,
Is far beyond a Prince's delicates:
His viands sparkling in a golden cup,
His body couched in a curious bed,
When Care, Mistrust, and Treason wait on him.

RICHARD THE SECOND

*King Richard the Second, another weak king with a soul of an artist,
indulges himself in a fantasy of arrogance and self-recrimination as he
defies his cousin, the usurper Henry Bolingbroke, from the walls of
Flint Castle, then surrenders himself as a prisoner and finally yields
him his crown in Westminster Hall before the great nobles of
England.* J.G.

Act III, Scene 3

KING:

We are amaz'd, and thus long have we stood
To watch the fearful bending of thy knee,
Because we thought ourself thy lawful King:
And if we be, how dare thy joints forget
To pay their awful duty to our presence?
If we be not, show us the Hand of God,
That hath dismiss'd us from our Stewardship,
For well we know, no hand of blood and bone
Can gripe the sacred handle of our Sceptre,

But that he do profane, steal, or usurp.
And though you think, that all, as you have done,
Have torn their souls, by turning them from us,
And we are barren, and bereft of friends:
Yet know, my Master, God Omnipotent,
Is mustering in the clouds, on our behalf,
Armies of Pestilence, and they shall strike
Your children yet unborn, and unbegot,
That lift your vassal hands against my head,
And threat the glory of my precious Crown.
Tell Bolingbroke, for yond methinks he stands
That every stride he makes upon my Land,
Is dangerous treason: He is come to ope
The purple testament of bleeding War;
But ere the Crown he look for, dwell in peace,
Ten thousand bloody crowns of mothers' sons
Shall ill become the flower of England's face,
Turn the complexion of her maid-pale Peace
To scarlet Indignation, and bedew
Her pastures' grass with faithful English blood. ....

Oh God, oh God, that e'er this tongue of mine,
That laid the sentence of dread banishment
On yond proud man, should take it off again
With words of sooth: Oh that I were as great
As is my grief, or lesser than my name,
Or that I could forget what I have been,
Or not remember what I must be now:
Swell'st thou proud heart? I'll give thee scope to
  beat,
Since foes have scope to beat both thee and me. ....

What must the King do now? must he submit?
The King shall do it: Must he be depos'd?
The King shall be contented: Must he lose
The name of King? o' God's name let it go.
I'll give my jewels for a set of beads,
My gorgeous Palace, for a hermitage,
My gay apparel, for an almsman's gown,
My figur'd goblets, for a dish of wood,
My sceptre, for a palmer's walking staff,
My subjects, for a pair of carved Saints,
And my large Kingdom, for a little grave,
A little little grave, an obscure grave.
Or I'll be buried in the King's high-way,
Some way of common trade, where subjects' feet
May hourly trample on their Sovereign's head:
For on my heart they tread whilst now, I live;
And buried once, why not upon my head? ....

Down, down I come, like glist'ring Phaeton,
Wanting the manage of unruly jades.
In the base court? base court, where Kings grow
  base,
To come at Traitors' call, and do them grace.
In the base court come down: down Court, down
  King,
For night-owls shriek, where mounting larks should
  sing.

Act IV, Scene I

Alack, why am I sent for to a King,
Before I have shook off the regal thoughts

Wherewith I reign'd? I hardly yet have learn'd
To insinuate, flatter, bow, and bend my knee.
Give Sorrow leave awhile, to tutor me
To this submission. Yet I well remember
The favours of these men: were they not mine?
Did they not sometime cry, All hail to me?
So Judas did to Christ: yet he in twelve,
Found truth in all, but one; I, in twelve thousand,
   none.
God save the King: will no man say, Amen?
Am I both Priest, and Clerk? Well then, Amen.
God save the King, although I be not he:
And yet Amen, if Heaven do think him me.
To do what service, am I sent for hither? ....

Give me the Crown. Here Cousin, seize the Crown:
Here Cousin, on this side my hand, and on that
   side yours.
Now is this golden Crown like a deep well,
That owes two buckets, filling one another,
The emptier ever dancing in the air,
The other down, unseen, and full of water:
That bucket down, and full of tears am I,
Drinking my griefs, whilst you mount up on
   high. ....

Now, mark me how I will undo myself.
I give this heavy weight from off my head,
And this unwieldy Sceptre from my hand,
The pride of kingly sway from out my heart.
With mine own tears I wash away my balm,

With mine own hands I give away my Crown,
With mine own tongue deny my sacred State,
With mine own breath release all duteous oaths;
All pomp and Majesty I do forswear:
My manors, rents, revenues I forgo;
My Acts, Decrees, and Statutes I deny:
God pardon all oaths that are broke to me,
God keep all oaths unbroke are made to thee.
Make me, that nothing have, with nothing griev'd,
And thou with all pleas'd, that hast all achiev'd.
Long mayst thou live in Richard's seat to sit,
And soon lie Richard in an earthy pit.
God save King Harry, un-king'd Richard says,
And send him many years of sunshine days. ....

Nay, all of you, that stand and look upon,
While that my misery doth bait myself,
Though some of you, with Pilate, wash your hands,
Showing an outward pity: yet you Pilates
Have here deliver'd me to my sour cross,
And water cannot wash away your sin. ....

Oh, that I were a mockery King of snow,
Standing before the sun of Bolingbroke,
To melt myself away in water-drops.
Good King, great King, and yet not greatly good,
And if my word be sterling still in England,
Let it command a mirror hither straight,
That it may show me what a face I have,
Since it is bankrupt of his Majesty. ....

Give me the glass, and therein will I read.
No deeper wrinkles yet? Hath Sorrow struck
So many blows upon this face of mine,
And left no deeper wounds? Oh flattering glass,
Like to my followers in prosperity,
Thou dost beguile me. Was this face, the face
That every day, under his household roof,
Did keep ten thousand men? Was this the face,
That like the Sun, did make beholders wink?
Was this the face, that fac'd so many follies,
And was at last out-fac'd by Bolingbroke?
A brittle glory shineth in this face,
As brittle as the glory, is the face,
For there it lies crack'd in a hundred shivers.
Mark, silent King, the moral of this sport,
How soon my sorrow hath destroy'd my face.

JULIUS CAESAR   Act I, Scene 2

*And now a jealous, unlucky man, the febrile Cassius tempting the
stoic Brutus to the murder of Julius Caesar.*   J. G.

CASSIUS:
    I cannot tell, what you and other men
    Think of this life: But for my single self,
    I had as lief not be, as live to be
    In awe of such a Thing, as I myself.
    I was born free as Caesar, so were you,
    We both have fed as well, and we can both

Endure the winter's cold, as well as he.
For once, upon a raw and gusty day,
The troubled Tiber, chafing with her shores,
Caesar said to me, Dar'st thou Cassius now
Leap in with me into this angry flood,
And swim to yonder point? Upon the word,
Accoutred as I was, I plunged in,
And bade him follow: so indeed he did.
The torrent roar'd, and we did buffet it
With lusty sinews, throwing it aside,
And stemming it with hearts of controversy.
But ere we could arrive the point propos'd,
Caesar cried, Help me Cassius, or I sink.
I (as Aeneas, our great ancestor,
Did from the flames of Troy, upon his shoulder
The old Anchises bear) so, from the waves of
  Tiber
Did I the tired Caesar: and this Man,
Is now become a God, and Cassius is
A wretched creature, and must bend his body,
If Caesar carelessly but nod on him.
He had a fever when he was in Spain,
And when the fit was on him, I did mark
How he did shake: 'Tis true, this God did shake,
His coward lips did from their colour fly,
And that same eye, whose bend doth awe the
  World,
Did lose his lustre: I did hear him groan:
Ay, and that tongue of his, that bade the Romans
Mark him, and write his speeches in their books,

Alas, it cried, Give me some drink Titinius,
As a sick girl: ye Gods, it doth amaze me,
A man of such a feeble temper should
So get the start of the majestic world,
And bear the palm alone. ....

Why man, he doth bestride the narrow world
Like a Colossus, and we petty men
Walk under his huge legs, and peep about
To find ourselves dishonourable graves.

HAMLET   Act II, Scene 2

*Hamlet, struggling to escape from the web of deceit and disillusion
with which he is surrounded, with his reason and passion in continual
conflict.*   J. G.

HAMLET:

Now I am alone.
Oh what a rogue and peasant slave am I!
Is it not monstrous that this Player here,
But in a fiction, in a dream of passion,
Could force his soul so to his own conceit,
That from its working, all his visage wann'd;
Tears in his eyes, distraction in 's aspect,
A broken voice, and his whole function suiting
With forms, to his conceit? and all for nothing?
For Hecuba?

What's Hecuba to him, or he to Hecuba,
That he should weep for her? What would he do,
Had he the motive and the cue for passion
That I have? He would drown the stage with tears,
And cleave the general ear with horrid speech:
Make mad the guilty, and appal the free,
Confound the ignorant, and amaze indeed,
The very faculties of eyes and ears. Yet I,
A dull and muddy-mettled rascal, peak
Like John-a-dreams, unpregnant of my cause,
And can say nothing: no, not for a King,
Upon whose property, and most dear life,
A damn'd defeat was made. Am I a coward?
Who calls me villain? breaks my pate across?
Plucks off my beard, and blows it in my face?
Tweaks me by th' nose? gives me the lie i' th' throat,
As deep as to the lungs? who does me this?
Ha? Swoons, I should take it: for it cannot be,
But I am pigeon-liver'd, and lack gall
To make oppression bitter, or ere this,
I should have fatted all the region kites
With this slave's offal, bloody, bawdy villain,
Remorseless, treacherous, lecherous, kindless villain!
O Vengeance!
Why, what an ass am I? This is most brave,
That I, the son of a dear father murdered,
Prompted to my revenge by Heaven, and Hell,
Must (like a whore) unpack my heart with words,
And fall a-cursing like a very drab.
A scullion! Fie upon't: foh. About my brain.

I have heard, that guilty creatures sitting at a play,
Have by the very cunning of the scene,
Been struck so to the soul, that presently
They have proclaim'd their malefactions.
For murder, though it have no tongue, will speak
With most miraculous organ. I'll have these Players,
Play something like the murder of my father,
Before mine uncle. I'll observe his looks,
I'll tent him to the quick: if he but blench
I know my course. This spirit that I have seen
May be the Devil, and the Devil hath power
To assume a pleasing shape, yea and perhaps
Out of my weakness, and my melancholy,
As he is very potent with such spirits,
Abuses me to damn me. I'll have grounds
More relative than this: the play's the thing,
Wherein I'll catch the conscience of the King.

Age

❧

DEATH   SICKNESS

MAN *against* HIMSELF

OLD AGE

TIME

THE STRAND that runs through the last section is death: sometimes directly, sometimes in the form of declining age, sometimes in the sheer weariness of life, sometimes in the fear of life to come. Once again we encounter that selfsame Henry IV who was the recipient of Hotspur's outburst and Richard II's histrionics. Now we encounter the man himself. He has deposed Richard and defeated Hotspur, but he stands fearful, conscious-stricken in a life of sleepless nights. His soliloquy could stand beside that of Henry VI. Both envy their simple subjects. But their natures are reflected in their speeches. One truly seeks the simple life; the other, temporary oblivion.

The next two passages are twined in a strange way. Macbeth is on his way to commit murder; Clarence dreams just before he is murdered. Both passages have a hallucinatory cast. Dream sequences are not infrequent in Shakespeare, and Clarence's passage is a vivid example of word-painting. There is a claustrophobic quality about his dream that the listener shares, and we are relieved as he is when he awakes to find himself alive. That Clarence later is actually drowned only arouses the original horror, and it is one of the touches that makes "Richard III" so strong a play.

Macbeth, prepared to murder Duncan, is neither asleep nor dreaming. But he seems to be in a hallucinatory state that resembles both. The scene is eerie, unreal; though the language and the images are precise enough, one has the feeling that everything is happening dimly and under water.

The three following passages, Claudio's from "Measure for Measure," Caesar's, and Hamlet's most famous soliloquy, have a unity of their own. All question the life to come: Claudio fearfully as befits a young man who has scarcely lived; Caesar nobly like a soldier to whom death is an everyday expectancy. Hamlet puts the matter most sensitively. He does not flinch from death as does Claudio, yet he comes to the same conclusion, that most of us will put up with the ills we have, rather than hasten to those we know nothing of. Or as Claudio puts it: "The weariest, and most loathed wordly life...is a paradise / To what we fear of death." Hamlet's statement has a philosophical sound to it. Although he has spoken more than once of suicide, no one quite believes that he is really prepared to do it. Claudio's short, blunt statement is less philosophical but more serious. For he faces imminent death and only the surrender of Isabella's chastity will save him. It is one of the great moments in the play, when the two meet and Claudio asks Isabella to weigh their respective losses. In the light of what may come, Claudio's brief statement takes on a dramatic force that the far more beautiful speech of Hamlet does not.

No Shakespeare anthology dealing with age and death would be complete without a representation from "King Lear," "the greatest play and the greatest poem in English," and Sir John has chosen one of the most moving and most piteous scenes in this most moving of plays: the scene of Lear's death beside the body of the daughter he has wronged. The wonders of the scene deserve scrutiny. The lines are abrupt, disjointed, reflecting the disarray of Lear's mind. Yet they have a logic of their own and an epigrammatic force. Nothing in Shakespeare compares with Lear's whispered words over the body of Cordelia, "Cordelia, Cordelia, stay a little." The fivefold repetition of "never" has a power greater than any more elaborate verbal amplification. And the sudden matter-of-fact stop in the middle of all his misery as he scrabbles to open the button at his neck is a touch of genius.

The final passages from the "The Tempest" relieve the somber tone of these selections. It is a play full of grace and grandeur, to use William Hazlitt's phrase. And the atmosphere of the island on which everything takes place can be gathered from the words of the earthbound Caliban which appear in the very first section, "Youth," in this anthology. Scholars have pointed out that after the dark mood of the tragedies, Shakespeare seems to have won through to a period marked by forgiveness and serenity, qualities embodied in "The Tempest." And some have taken the speech beginning "Our revels now are ended," with its reference to the Globe, the name of Shakespeare's theater, as the poet's farewell to his labors as a playwright. It is almost as if he had concluded with the words of one of his own characters: "Men must endure their going hence, even as their coming hither. Ripeness is all."

T. L.

SONNET 138

When my love swears that she is made of truth,
I do believe her, though I know she lies,
That she may think me some untutor'd youth
Unlearned in the world's false subtilties.
Thus vainly thinking that she thinks me young,
Although she knows my days are past the best,
Simply I credit her false-speaking tongue;
On both sides thus is simple truth suppress'd.
But wherefore says she not she is unjust?
And wherefore say not I that I am old?
O, love's best habit is in seeming trust,
And age in love loves not to have years told.
    Therefore I lie with her and she with me,
    And in our faults by lies we flatter'd be.

SONNET 30

When to the sessions of sweet silent thought
I summon up remembrance of things past,
I sigh the lack of many a thing I sought
And with old woes new wail my dear time's waste;
Then can I drown an eye unus'd to flow,
For precious friends hid in death's dateless night,
And weep afresh love's long since cancell'd woe,
And moan th' expense of many a vanish'd sight;
Then can I grieve at grievances foregone,
And heavily from woe to woe tell o'er
The sad account of fore-bemoaned moan,
Which I new pay as if not paid before:

But if the while I think on thee, dear friend,
All losses are restor'd and sorrows end.

SONNET 73

That time of year thou mayst in me behold
When yellow leaves, or none, or few, do hang
Upon those boughs which shake against the cold,
Bare ruin'd choirs, where late the sweet birds sang:
In me thou see'st the twilight of such day
As after sunset fadeth in the west;
Which by and by black night doth take away,
Death's second self, that seals up all in rest:
In me thou see'st the glowing of such fire,
That on the ashes of his youth doth lie,
As the death-bed whereon it must expire,
Consum'd with that which it was nourish'd by.
   This thou perceiv'st, which makes thy love more
     strong,
   To love that well which thou must leave ere long.

HENRY THE FOURTH (Part 2)   Act III, Scene 1

Shakespeare did not live to be an old man and we know very little of his personal life, of the agonies and distresses which he himself experienced. Certainly no poet has ever written more poignantly of the agony of madness, the guilt of conscience or the black despair of sleepless nights. Henry the Fourth, that same Bolingbroke who'd opposed King Richard and had him put to death, is haunted in sickness and old age by sleeplessness and remorse.   J.G.

HENRY:

How many thousand of my poorest subjects
Are at this hour asleep? O Sleep, O gentle Sleep,
Nature's soft nurse, how have I frighted thee,
That thou no more wilt weigh mine eyelids down,
And steep my senses in forgetfulness?
Why rather, Sleep, liest thou in smoky cribs,
Upon uneasy pallets stretching thee,
And hush'd with buzzing night-flies to thy slumber,
Than in the perfum'd chambers of the great,
Under the canopies of costly state,
And lull'd with sounds of sweetest melody?
O thou dull God, why liest thou with the vile,
In loathsome beds, and leav'st the kingly couch,
A watch-case, or a common 'larum-bell?
Wilt thou, upon the high and giddy mast,
Seal up the ship-boy's eyes, and rock his brains,
In cradle of the rude imperious surge,
And in the visitation of the winds,
Who take the ruffian billows by the top,
Curling their monstrous heads, and hanging them
With deaf'ning clamour in the slipp'ry clouds,
That with the hurly, Death itself awakes?
Canst thou, O partial Sleep, give thy repose
To the wet sea-boy, in an hour so rude:
And in the calmest, and most stillest night,
With all appliances, and means to boot,
Deny it to a King? Then happy low, lie down,
Uneasy lies the head, that wears a crown.

MACBETH   Act II, Scene 1

Macbeth, prepared for the murder of Duncan, comes into the empty
courtyard with his servant.   J. G.

MACBETH:

Go bid thy Mistress, when my drink is ready,
She strike upon the bell. Get thee to bed.
Is this a dagger, that I see before me,
The handle toward my hand? Come, let me clutch
   thee:
I have thee not, and yet I see thee still.
Art thou not, fatal vision, sensible
To feeling, as to sight? or art thou but
A dagger of the mind, a false creation,
Proceeding from the heat-oppressed brain?
I see thee yet, in form as palpable,
As this which now I draw.
Thou marshall'st me the way that I was going,
And such an instrument I was to use.
Mine eyes are made the fools o' th' other senses,
Or else worth all the rest: I see thee still;
And on thy blade, and dudgeon, gouts of blood,
Which was not so before. There's no such thing:
It is the bloody business, which informs
Thus to mine eyes. Now o'er the one half-world
Nature seems dead, and wicked dreams abuse
The curtain'd sleep: witchcraft celebrates
Pale Hecat's offerings: and wither'd Murther,
Alarum'd by his sentinel, the wolf,
Whose howl's his watch, thus with his stealthy pace,

With Tarquin's ravishing stride, towards his design
Moves like a ghost. Thou sure and firm-set Earth
Hear not my steps, which way they walk, for fear
Thy very stones prate of my whereabout,
And take the present horror from the time,
Which now suits with it. Whiles I threat, he lives:
Words to the heat of deeds too cold breath gives.
I go, and it is done: the bell invites me.
Hear it not, Duncan, for it is a knell,
That summons thee to Heaven, or to Hell.

RICHARD THE THIRD   Act I, Scene 4

*And the wretched guilt-haunted Clarence in RICHARD THE THIRD,
so soon to be murdered by his brother Richard, Duke of Gloucester,
wakes in terror in his cell in the Tower of London where he has been
imprisoned.*   J.G.

CLARENCE:

O, I have passed a miserable night,
So full of fearful dreams, of ugly sights,
That as I am a Christian faithful man,
I would not spend another such a night
Though 'twere to buy a world of happy days:
So full of dismal terror was the time. ....

Me thought that I had broken from the Tower,
And was embark'd to cross to Burgundy,
And in my company my Brother Gloucester,

Who from my cabin tempted me to walk,
Upon the hatches: Thence we look'd toward
  England,
And cited up a thousand heavy times,
During the wars of York and Lancaster
That had befallen us. As we pac'd along
Upon the giddy footing of the hatches,
Me thought that Gloucester stumbled, and in falling
Struck me (that sought to stay him) overboard,
Into the tumbling billows of the main.
Lord, Lord, me thought what pain it was to drown,
What dreadful noise of water in mine ears,
What ugly sights of death within mine eyes.
Me thought, I saw a thousand fearful wracks:
Ten thousand men that fishes gnaw'd upon:
Wedges of gold, great anchors, heaps of pearl,
Inestimable stones, unvalued jewels,
All scatter'd in the bottom of the sea,
Some lay in dead-men's skulls, and in those holes
Where eyes did once inhabit, there were crept
(As 'twere in scorn of eyes) reflecting gems,
That woo'd the slimy bottom of the deep,
And mock'd the dead bones that lay scatter'd by. ....

Full often did I strive
To yield the ghost: but still the envious flood
Kept in my soul, and would not let it forth
To seek the empty, vast, and wand'ring air:
But smother'd it within my panting bulk,
Which almost burst, to belch it in the sea. ....

O then, began the tempest to my soul.
I passed (me thought) the Melancoly Flood,
With that grim Ferry-man which poets write of,
Unto the Kingdom of perpetual Night.
The first that there did greet my stranger-soul,
Was my great Father-in-Law, renowned Warwick,
Who cried aloud: What scourge for perjury,
Can this dark Monarchy afford false Clarence?
And so he vanish'd. Then came wand'ring by,
A shadow like an angel, with bright hair
Dabbled in blood, and he shriek'd out aloud
Clarence is come, false, fleeting, perjur'd Clarence,
That stabb'd me in the field by Tewkesbury:
Seize on him Furies, take him to your torments.
With that (me thought) a legion of foul fiends
Environ'd me, and howled in mine ears
Such hideous cries, that with the very noise,
I (trembling) wak'd, and for a season after,
Could not believe, but that I was in Hell,
Such terrible impression made my dream.

MEASURE FOR MEASURE   Act III, Scene 1

_In_ MEASURE FOR MEASURE, _the young Claudio, condemned for
fornication, cries out in horror at his cruel fate._   J.G.

CLAUDIO:

Ay, but to die, and go we know not where,
To lie in cold obstruction, and to rot,
This sensible warm motion, to become
A kneaded clod; And the delighted spirit
To bathe in fiery floods, or to reside
In thrilling region of thick-ribbed ice,
To be imprison'd in the viewless winds
And blown with restless violence round about
The pendent world: or to be worse than worst
Of those, that lawless and incertain thought,
Imagine howling, 'tis too horrible.
The weariest, and most loathed worldly life
That age, ache, penury, and imprisonment
Can lay on nature, is a paradise
To what we fear of death.

JULIUS CAESAR   Act II, Scene 2

*But Julius Caesar, superstitious, cold, arrogant, can silence his young
wife's fears and pleadings with a fine reproof.*   J.G.

CAESAR:

Cowards die many times before their deaths,
The valiant never taste of death but once:
Of all the wonders that I yet have heard,
It seems to me most strange that men should fear,
Seeing that death, a necessary end
Will come, when it will come.

HAMLET

Hamlet, in his black clothes, might seem to be the death figure par excellence in Shakespeare. Yet how simply he speaks when he's faced with the great issues of life and death.   J. G.

Act II, Scene 2

HAMLET:

I have of late, and wherefore know not, lost all my
mirth, forgone all custom of exercises; and indeed, it
goes so heavily with my disposition; that this goodly
frame the earth, seems to me a sterile promontory;
this most excellent canopy the air, look you, this
brave o'er-hanging firmament, this majestical roof,
fretted with golden fire: why, it seems no other thing
to me, than a foul and pestilent congregation of
vapours. What a piece of work is man! how noble in
reason! how infinite in faculty! in form and moving
how express and admirable! in action, how like an
angel! in apprehension, how like a god! the beauty of
the world, the paragon of animals; and yet to me,
what is this quintessence of dust? man delights not
me; no, nor woman neither; though by your smiling
you would seem to say so.

Act III, Scene 1

HAMLET:

To be, or not to be, that is the question:
Whether 'tis nobler in the mind to suffer

The slings and arrows of outrageous Fortune,
Or to take arms against a sea of troubles,
And by opposing end them: to die to sleep;
No more; and by a sleep, to say we end
The heart-ache, and the thousand natural shocks
That flesh is heir to? 'tis a consummation
Devoutly to be wish'd. To die, to sleep,
To sleep, perchance to dream; ay, there's the rub,
For in that sleep of death, what dreams may come,
When we have shuffled off this mortal coil,
Must give us pause. There's the respect
That makes calamity of so long life:
For who would bear the whips and scorns of time,
The oppressor's wrong, the proud man's contumely,
The pangs of dispriz'd love, the Law's delay,
The insolence of office, and the spurns
Which patient merit of the unworthy takes,
When he himself might his quietus make,
With a bare bodkin? who would fardels bear,
To grunt and sweat under a weary life,
But that the dread of something after death,
The undiscover'd country, from whose bourn
No traveller returns, puzzles the will,
And makes us rather bear those ills we have,
Than fly to others that we know not of.
Thus conscience doth make cowards of us all,
And thus the native hue of resolution
Is sicklied o'er with the pale cast of thought,
And enterprises of great pitch and moment,
With this regard their currents turn awry,
And lose the name of action.

Act V, Scene 2

HAMLET:

But thou wouldst not think how ill all's here about my heart: but it is no matter. ....

It is but foolery; it is such a kind of gain-giving, as would perhaps trouble a woman. ....

Not a whit, we defy augury; there's a special providence in the fall of a sparrow. If it be now, 'tis not to come: if it be not to come, it will be now: if it be not now, yet it will come; the readiness is all, since no man hath aught of what he leaves. What is't to leave betimes? Let be.

SONNET 29

When in disgrace with fortune and men's eyes,
I all alone beweep my outcast state,
And trouble deaf heaven with my bootless cries,
And look upon myself and curse my fate,
Wishing me like to one more rich in hope,
Featur'd like him, like him with friends possess'd,
Desiring this man's art, and that man's scope,
With what I most enjoy contented least;
Yet in these thoughts myself almost despising,
Haply I think on thee, and then my state,
Like to the lark at break of day arising
From sullen earth, sings hymns at heaven's gate;
    For thy sweet love rememb'red such wealth brings
    That then I scorn to change my state with kings.

CYMBELINE

The dirge from CYMBELINE, *spoken by the young princes over the supposed corpse of their play-fellow, their sister, Imogen.*

J. G.

GUIDERIUS: Fear no more the heat o' th' Sun,
Nor the furious Winter's rages,
Thou thy worldly task hast done,
Home art gone, and ta'en thy wages.
Golden Lads, and Girls all must,
As Chimney-sweepers come to dust.

ARVIRAGUS: Fear no more the frown o' th' Great.
Thou art past the Tyrant's stroke,
Care no more to clothe and eat,
To thee the reed is as the oak:
   The scepter, learning, physick must,
   All follow this and come to dust.

GUIDERIUS: Fear no more the lightning flash.
ARVIRAGUS: Nor th' all dreaded thunderstone.
GUIDERIUS: Fear not slander, censure rash.
ARVIRAGUS: Thou hast finish'd joy and moan.
BOTH: All Lovers young, all Lovers must,
Consign to thee and come to dust.

GUIDERIUS: No Exorciser harm thee,
ARVIRAGUS: Nor no witch-craft charm thee
GUIDERIUS: Ghost unlaid forbear thee.
ARVIRAGUS: Nothing ill come near thee.
BOTH: Quiet consummation have,
And renowned be thy grave.

ROMEO AND JULIET   Act V, Scene 3

*Two contrasting death scenes of youth and age. The boy Romeo,
standing in the dark vault of the Capulets with the poison in his hand,
seems to have become a grown man at last, as he gazes on Juliet for the
last time.*   J.G.

ROMEO:

How oft when men are at the point of death,
Have they been merry! which their keepers call
A lightning before death: O how may I
Call this a lightning! O my Love, my wife,
Death that hath suck'd the honey of thy breath,
Hath had no power yet upon thy beauty:
Thou art not conquer'd, beauty's ensign yet
Is crimson in thy lips and in thy cheeks,
And death's pale flag is not advanced there.
Tybalt liest thou there in thy bloody sheet?
O what more favour can I do to thee,
Than with that hand which cut thy youth in twain,
To sunder his that was thine enemy?
Forgive me cousin. Ah dear Juliet
Why art thou yet so fair? Shall I believe
That unsubstantial death is amorous,
And that the lean abhorred monster keeps
Thee here in dark to be his paramour?
For fear of that I still will stay with thee,
And never from this palace of dim night
Depart again: here, here will I remain,
With worms that are thy chamber-maids: O here
Will I set up my everlasting rest:

And shake the yoke of inauspicious stars,
From this world-wearied flesh: eyes look your last:
Arms take your last embrace: and lips, O you
The doors of breath, seal with a righteous kiss
A dateless bargain to engrossing death:
Come bitter conduct, come unsavoury guide,
Thou desperate pilot, now at once run on
The dashing rocks, thy sea-sick weary bark:
Here's to my love. O true apothecary:
Thy drugs are quick. Thus with a kiss I die.

KING LEAR   Act V, Scene 3

*But King Lear, stretched on the ground beside the hanged body of his
wronged daughter Cordelia, dies like a little child again.*   J.G.

LEAR:

Howl, howl, howl, howl: O you men of stone,
Had I your tongues and eyes, I'ld use them so,
That Heaven's vault should crack: she's gone for
   ever.
I know when one is dead, and when one lives, ...

She's dead as earth: lend me a looking-glass,
If that her breath do mist or stain the stone,
Why then she lives. ....

This feather stirs, she lives: if it be so,
It is a chance that does redeem all sorrows
That ever I have felt. ....

A plague upon you murderers, traitors all,
I might have sav'd her, now she's gone forever.
Cordelia, Cordelia, stay a little. Ha:
What is't thou say'st? Her voice was ever soft,
Gentle, and low, an excellent thing in woman.
I kill'd the slave that was a-hanging thee. ....

And my poor fool is hang'd: no, no, no life?
Why should a horse, a dog, a rat, have life,
And thou no breath at all? Thou'lt come no more,
Never, never, never, never, never.
Pray you undo this button. Thank you sir,
Do you see this? Look on her? look her lips,
Look there, look there. ....

THE TEMPEST

And lastly Prospero, the magician of THE TEMPEST, dismisses the masque which he has evoked for the wedding of the two young people, his daughter and Ferdinand, and later invokes the spirits of the island for the last time and renounces his wizardry forever and finally speaks an epilogue to the audience. J.G.

Act IV, Scene 1

PROSPERO:

Our revels now are ended: these our actors
(As I foretold you) were all spirits, and
Are melted into air, into thin air,
And like the baseless fabric of this vision,

The cloud-capp'd Towers, the gorgeous Palaces,
The solemn Temples, the great Globe itself,
Yea, all which it inherit, shall dissolve,
And like this insubstantial pageant faded
Leave not a rack behind: we are such stuff
As dreams are made on; and our little life
Is rounded with a sleep.

Act V, Scene 1

Ye elves of hills, brooks, standing lakes and
    groves,
And ye that on the sands with printless foot
Do chase the ebbing Neptune, and do fly him
When he comes back; you demi-puppets, that
By moonshine do the green sour ringlets make,
Whereof the ewe not bites: and you, whose
    pastime
Is to make midnight mushrooms, that rejoice
To hear the solemn curfew, by whose aid
(Weak masters though ye be) I have bedimm'd
The noontide Sun, call'd forth the mutinous winds,
And 'twixt the green sea, and the azur'd vault
Set roaring war: to the dread rattling thunder
Have I given fire, and rifted Jove's stout oak
With his own bolt: the strong-bas'd promontory
Have I made shake, and by the spurs pluck'd up
The pine and cedar. Graves at my command
Have wak'd their sleepers, op'd, and let 'em forth
By my so potent Art. But this rough magic
I here abjure: and when I have requir'd

Some heavenly music (which even now I do)
To work mine end upon their senses, that
This airy charm is for, I'll break my staff,
Bury it certain fathoms in the earth,
And deeper than did ever plummet sound
I'll drown my book.

Epilogue:

Now my charms are all o'erthrown,
And what strength I have's mine own.
Which is most faint: now 'tis true
I must be here confin'd by you,
Or sent to Naples; let me not,
Since I have my Dukedom got,
And pardon'd the deceiver, dwell
In this bare Island, by your spell,
But release me from my bands
With the help of your good hands:
Gentle breath of yours, my sails
Must fill, or else my project fails,
Which was to please: now I want
Spirits to enforce, Art to enchant:
And my ending is despair,
Unless I be reliev'd by prayer
Which pierces so, that it assaults
Mercy itself, and frees all faults.
    As you from crimes would pardon'd be,
    Let your indulgence set me free.

Thomas Lask has been a member of the Book Review staff of The New York Times, edited The New York Times Book of Verse, and taught English for many years at The City College of New York. He is now Assistant Cultural News Editor of the Times.

THE WORKS OF SHAKESPEARE

PLAYS

APPROXIMATE DATE		FIRST PRINTED
Before 1594	HENRY VI *three parts*	*Folio* 1623
	RICHARD III	1597
	TITUS ANDRONICUS	1594
	LOVE'S LABOUR'S LOST	1598
	THE TWO GENTLEMEN OF VERONA	*Folio*
	THE COMEDY OF ERRORS	*Fiolo*
	THE TAMING OF THE SHREW	*Folio*
1594-1597	ROMEO AND JULIET *(pirated 1597)*	1599
	A MIDSUMMER NIGHT'S DREAM	1600
	RICHARD II	1597
	KING JOHN	*Folio*
	THE MERCHANT OF VENICE	1600
1597-1600	HENRY IV *part i*	1598
	HENRY IV *part ii*	1600
	HENRY V *(pirated 1600)*	*Folio*
	MUCH ADO ABOUT NOTHING	1600
	MERRY WIVES OF WINDSOR *(pirated 1602)*	*Folio*
	AS YOU LIKE IT	*Folio*
	JULIUS CAESAR	*Folio*
	TROYLUS AND CRESSIDA *(pirated 1603)*	1609
1601-1608	HAMLET	1604
	TWELFTH NIGHT	*Folio*
	MEASURE FOR MEASURE	*Folio*
	ALL'S WELL THAT ENDS WELL	*Folio*
	OTHELLO	1622
	LEAR	1608
	MACBETH	*Folio*
	TIMON OF ATHENS	*Folio*
	ANTHONY AND CLEOPATRA	*Folio*
	CORIOLANUS	*Folio*
After 1608	PERICLES *(omitted from the Folio)*	1609
	CYMBELINE	*Folio*
	THE WINTER'S TALE	*Folio*
	THE TEMPEST	*Folio*
	HENRY VIII	*Folio*

POEMS

DATE UNKNOWN		
	VENUS AND ADONIS	1593
	THE RAPE OF LUCRECE	1594
	SONNETS } A LOVER'S COMPLAINT	1609
	THE PHOENIX AND THE TURTLE	1601

WILLIAM SHAKESPEARE

William Shakespeare was born at Stratford upon Avon in April, 1564. He was the third child, and eldest son, of John Shakespeare and Mary Arden. His father was one of the most prosperous men of Stratford, who held in turn the chief offices in the town. His mother was of gentle birth, the daughter of Robert Arden of Wilmcote. In December, 1582, Shakespeare married Ann Hathaway, daughter of a farmer of Shottery, near Stratford; their first child Susanna was baptized on May 6, 1583, and twins, Hamnet and Judith, on February 22, 1585. Little is known of Shakespeare's early life; but it is unlikely that a writer who dramatized such an incomparable range and variety of human kinds and experiences should have spent his early manhood entirely in placid pursuits in a country town. There is one tradition, not universally accepted, that he fled from Stratford because he was in trouble for deer stealing, and had fallen foul of Sir Thomas Lucy, the local magnate; another that he was for some time a schoolmaster.

From 1592 onwards the records are much fuller. In March, 1592, the Lord Strange's players produced a new play at the Rose Theatre called *Harry the Sixth*, which was very successful, and·was probably the *First Part of Henry VI*. In the autumn of 1592 Robert Greene, the best known of the professional writers, as he was dying wrote a letter to three fellow writers in which he warned them against the ingratitude of players in general, and in particular against an 'upstart crow' who 'supposes he is as much able to bombast out a blank verse as the best of you: and being an absolute Johannes Factotum is in his own conceit the only Shakespeare in a country.' This is the first reference to Shakespeare, and the whole passage suggests that Shakespeare had become suddenly famous as a playwright. At this time Shakespeare was brought into touch with Edward Alleyne the great tragedian, and Christopher Marlowe, whose thundering parts of Tamburlaine, the Jew of Malta, and Dr. Faustus Alleyne was acting, as well as Hieronimo, the hero of Kyd's *Spanish Tragedy,* the most famous of all Elizabethan plays.

In April, 1593, Shakespeare published his poem *Venus and Adonis,* which was dedicated to the young Earl of Southampton: it was a great and lasting success, and was reprinted nine times in the next few years. In May, 1594, his second poem, *The Rape of Lucrece*, was also dedicated to Southampton.

There was little playing in 1593, for the theatres were shut during a severe outbreak of the plague; but in the autumn of 1594, when the plague ceased, the playing companies were reorganized, and Shakespeare became a sharer in the Lord Chamberlain's company who went to play in the Theatre in Shoreditch. During these months Marlowe and Kyd had died. Shakespeare was thus for a time without a rival. He had already written the three parts of *Henry VI, Richard III, Titus Andronicus, The Two Gentlemen of Verona, Love's Labour's Lost, the Comedy of Errors,* and *The Taming of the Shrew.* Soon afterwards he wrote the first of his greater plays —*Romeo and Juliet*—and he followed this success in the next three years with *A Midsummer Night's Dream, Richard II,* and *The Merchant of Venice.* The two parts of *Henry IV,* introducing Falstaff, the most popular of all his comic characters, were written in 1597-8.

The company left the Theatre in 1597 owing to disputes over a renewal of the ground lease, and went to play at the Curtain in the same neighbourhood. The disputes continued throughout 1598, and at Christmas the players settled the matter by demolishing the old Theatre and re-erecting a new playhouse on the South bank of the Thames, near Southwark Cathedral. This playhouse was named the Globe. The expenses of the new building were shared by the chief members of the Company, including Shakespeare, who was now a man of some means. In 1596 he had bought New Place, a large house in the centre of Stratford, for £60, and through his father purchased a coat-of-arms from the Heralds, which was the official recognition that he and his family were gentlefolk.

By the summer of 1598 Shakespeare was recognized as the greatest of English dramatists, Booksellers were printing his more popular plays, at times even in pirated or stolen versions, and he received a remarkable tribute from a young writer named Francis Meres, in his book *Palladis Tamia.* In a long catalogue of English authors Meres gave Shakespeare more prominence than any other writer, and mentioned by name twelve of his plays.

Shortly before the Globe was opened, Shakespeare had completed the cycle of plays dealing with the whole story of the Wars of the Roses with

Henry V. It was followed by *As You Like it,* and *Julius Caesar,* the first of the maturer tragedies. In the next three years he wrote *Troilus and Cressida, The Merry Wives of Windsor, Hamlet,* and *Twelfth Night.*

On March 24, 1603, Queen Elizabeth died. The company had often performed before her, but they found her successor a far more enthusiastic patron. One of the first acts of King James was to take over the company and to promote them to be his own servants, so that henceforward they were known as the King's Men. They acted now very frequently at Court, and prospered accordingly. In the early years of the reign Shakespeare wrote the more sombre comedies, *All's Well that Ends Well,* and *Measure for Measure,* which were followed by *Othello, Macbeth,* and *King Lear.* Then he returned to Roman themes with *Antony and Cleopatra* and *Coriolanus.*

Since 1601 Shakespeare had been writing less, and there were now a number of rival dramatists who were introducing new styles of drama, particularly Ben Jonson (whose first successful comedy, *Every Man in his Humour,* was acted by Shakespeare's company in 1598), Chapman, Dekker, Marston, and Beaumont and Fletcher who began to write in 1607. In 1608 the King's Men acquired a second playhouse, an indoor private theatre in the fashionable quarter of the Blackfriars. At private theatres, plays were performed indoors; the prices charged were higher than in the public playhouses, and the audience consequently was more select. Shakespeare seems to have retired from the stage about this time: his name does not occur in the various lists of players after 1607. Henceforward he lived for the most part at Stratford, where he was regarded as one of the most important citizens. He still wrote a few plays, and he tried his hand at the new form of tragi-comedy—a play with tragic incidents but a happy ending—which Beaumont and Fletcher had popularized. He wrote four of these—*Pericles, Cymbeline, The Winter's Tale,* and *The Tempest,* which was acted at Court in 1611. For the last four years of his life he lived in retirement. His son Hamnet had died in 1596: his two daughters were now married. Shakespeare died at Stratford upon Avon on April 23, 1616, and was buried in the chancel of the church, before the high altar. Shortly afterwards a memorial which still exists, with a portrait bust, was set up on the North wall. His wife survived him.

When Shakespeare died fourteen of his plays had been separately published in Quarto booklets. In 1623 his surviving fellow actors, John

Heming and Henry Condell, with the co-operation of a number of printers, published a collected edition of thirty-six plays in one Folio volume, with an engraved portrait, memorial verses by Ben Jonson and others, and an Epistle to the Reader in which Heming and Condell make the interesting note that Shakespeare's 'hand and mind together, and what he thought, he uttered with that easiness that we have scarce received from him a blot in his papers.'

The plays as printed in the Quartos or the Folio differ considerably from the usual modern text. They are often not divided into scenes, and sometimes not even into acts. Nor are there place-headings at the beginning of each scene, because in the Elizabethan theatre there was no scenery.

G.B. HARRISON

RECORDINGS AVAILABLE FROM CAEDMON

AS YOU LIKE IT

Performance by Vanessa Redgrave, Keith Michell, Max Adrian, Stanley Holloway.
This recording, complete on three records, contains the text of the play, edited by the prominent authority G. B. Harrison. Directed by Peter Wood. Music arranged by Neville Marriner.
SRS 210 3-12" LPs $23.94 CDL 5210 3 cassettes $23.94

CYMBELINE

Performance by Claire Bloom, Boris Karloff, Pamela Brown.
The text, edited by the prominent authority G. B. Harrison, is included. Directed by Howard Sackler.
SRS 236 3-12" LPs $23.94 CDL 5236 3 cassettes $23.94

HAMLET

Performance by Paul Scofield, Diana Wynyard, Wilfrid Lawson, Zena Walker.
The text, edited by the prominent authority G. B. Harrison, is included. Directed by Howard Sackler.
SRS 232 4-12" LPs $31.92 CDL 5232 4 cassettes $31.92

JULIUS CAESAR

Performance by Sir Ralph Richardson, Anthony Quayle, John Mills, Alan Bates.
The text, edited by the prominent authority G. B. Harrison, is included. Directed by Howard Sackler.
SRS 230 3-12" LPs $23.94 CDL 5230 3 cassettes $23.94

KING HENRY THE FIFTH

Performance by Ian Holm, Charles Gray, Ian McKellan, Janet Suzman, Bernard Bresslaw, John Laurie, Sir John Gielgud.
The complete text, edited by the prominent authority G. B. Harrison, is included. Directed by Howard Sackler. Music composed and conducted by Marc Wilkinson.
SRS 219 4-12" LPs $31.92 CDL 5219 4 cassettes $31.92

KING HENRY THE FOURTH, PART ONE

Performance by Harry Andrews, Pamela Brown, Dame Edith Evans, Richard Johnson, Ronald Lewis, Anthony Quayle, Sir Michael Redgrave.
The text, edited by the prominent authority G. B. Harrison, is included. Directed by Peter Wood. Music by Wilfred Josephs.
SRS 217 3-12" LPs $23.94 CDL 5217 3 cassettes $23.94

KING HENRY THE FOURTH, PART TWO

Performance by Max Adrian, Harry Andrews, Sir Felix Aylmer, Pamela Brown, Dame Edith Evans, Richard Johnson, Miles Malleson, Anthony Quayle, Joyce Redman.

The complete text, edited by the prominent authority G. B. Harrison, is included. Musical supervisor Neville Marriner.
SRS 218 4-12" LPs $31.92 CDL 5218 4 cassettes $31.92

KING LEAR
Performance by Paul Scofield, Rachel Roberts, Pamela Brown, Cyril Cusack, Robert Stephens.
The text, edited by the prominent authority G. B. Harrison, is included.
Directed by Howard Sackler.
SRS 233 4-12" LPs $31.92 CDL 5233 4 cassettes $31.92

KING RICHARD THE SECOND
Performance by Sir John Gielgud, Keith Michell, Leo McKern, Michael Hordern.
The complete text, edited by the prominent authority G. B. Harrison, is included. Directed by Peter Wood.
SRS 216 3-12" LPs $23.94 CDL 5216 3 cassettes $23.94

KING RICHARD THE THIRD
Performance by Robert Stephens, Dame Peggy Ashcroft, Cyril Cusack, Ian Holm, Jeremy Brett, Glenda Jackson, Nigel Davenport.
The complete text, edited by the prominent authority G. B. Harrison, is included. Directed by Howard Sackler.
SRS 223 4-12" LPs $31.92 CDL 5210 4 cassettes $31.92

LOVE'S LABOUR'S LOST
Performance by Geraldine McEwan, Jeremy Brett, Ian Holm, Ian Richardson.
A complete text edited by the prominent authority G. B. Harrison is included.
Directed by Peter Wood.
SRS 207 3-12" LPs $23.94 CDL 5207 3 cassettes $23.94

MACBETH
Performance by Anthony Quayle, Gwen Ffrangcon-Davies, Stanley Holloway, Robert Hardy, Ian Holm, Alec McCowen.
The text, edited by the prominent authority G. B. Harrison, is included.
Directed by Howard Sackler.
SRS 231 3-12" LPs $23.94 CDL 5231 3 cassettes $23.94

MEASURE FOR MEASURE
Performance by Sir John Gielgud, Margaret Leighton, Sir Ralph Richardson, Mark Dignam, Tony White, Alec McCowen.
The complete text, edited by the prominent authority G. B. Harrison, is included. Directed by Peter Wood.
SRS 204 3-12" LPs $23.94 CDL 5204 3 cassettes $23.94

THE MERCHANT OF VENICE
Performance by Hugh Griffith, Dorothy Tutin, Harry Andrews.
The text edited by the prominent authority G. B. Harrison, is included.
Directed by Peter Wood.
SRS 209 2-12" LPs $15.96 CDL 5209 2 cassettes $15.96

A MIDSUMMER NIGHT'S DREAM
Performance by Paul Scofield, Joy Parker, Barbara Jefford, John Stride,
Jack Gwillim, Miles Malleson, Edward De Souza.
The text of the play is edited by the prominent authority G. B. Harrison.
Directed by Howard Sackler.
SRS 208 3-12" LPs $23.94 CDL 5208 3 cassettes $23.94

MUCH ADO ABOUT NOTHING
Performance by Rex Harrison, Rachel Roberts, Alan Webb, Charles Gray,
Robert Stephens.
The three-record set comes with the complete text of the play, edited by the
prominent authority G. B. Harrison. Directed by Howard Sackler.
SRS 206 3-12" LPs $23.94 CDL 5206 3 cassettes $23.94

ROMEO AND JULIET
Performance by Claire Bloom, Dame Edith Evans, Albert Finney.
The complete text, edited by the prominent authority G. B. Harrison, is
included. Directed by Howard Sackler.
SRS 228 3-12" LPs $23.94 CDL 5228 3 cassettes $23.94

SONNETS
Performance by Sir John Gielgud
The complete text, edited by the prominent authority G. B. Harrison, is
included. Directed by Howard Sackler.
SRS 241 2-12" LPs $15.96 CDL 5241 2 cassettes $15.96

THE TEMPEST
Performance by Sir Michael Redgrave, Hugh Griffith, Vanessa Redgrave,
Anna Massey, Alec McCowen.
The complete text, edited by the prominent authority G. B. Harrison, is
included. Directed by Peter Wood. Incidental music by Wilfred Josephs.
Musical supervisor Neville Marriner.
SRS 201 3-12" LPs $23.94 CDL 5201 3 cassettes $23.94

THE WINTER'S TALE
Performance by Sir John Gielgud, Dame Peggy Ashcroft, George Rose.
Complete with text, edited by the prominent authority G. B. Harrison.
Directed by Peter Wood. Music for songs and dances by Christopher Fry.
SRS 214 3-12" LPs $23.94 CDL 5214 3 cassettes $23.94